MW01713926

Changing State

John Stringer

The children saw a puddle of water in the yard. An hour later, the puddle was smaller. An hour after that, the puddle had gone. The yard was dry. Where had the water gone?

The children had ideas. One thought the water had sunk into the yard. Another thought an animal had drunk it. Others thought the water had gone up into the sky. Who was right?

The children wet a small towel. They found its mass. They hung it on a line. Every hour, the children weighed the towel again. They found that its mass changed. Every hour, the towel had less mass. The towel was losing water. Where was the water going?

The towel had dried out. It had lost all the water. The water had evaporated. Liquids lose droplets as vapour. Droplets of **water vapour** had been lost from the towel. The droplets had gone into the air. We call this **evaporation**. The droplets evaporate.

The water from the puddle in the yard had evaporated.

There are droplets of water in the air all around us. Sometimes, there are so many droplets that we can see them as a cloud of steam. These droplets may collect on a cold surface. The water vapour becomes a liquid again. We call this **condensation**. The droplets condense.

Condensation is the opposite of evaporation. Water evaporates from the sea, from streams and rivers. The water vapour rises into the air.

The water vapour condenses. It forms clouds of water vapour in the sky. Droplets of water may run together and form drops. These drops may fall as rain. The picture shows how water circulates between air, land and sea.

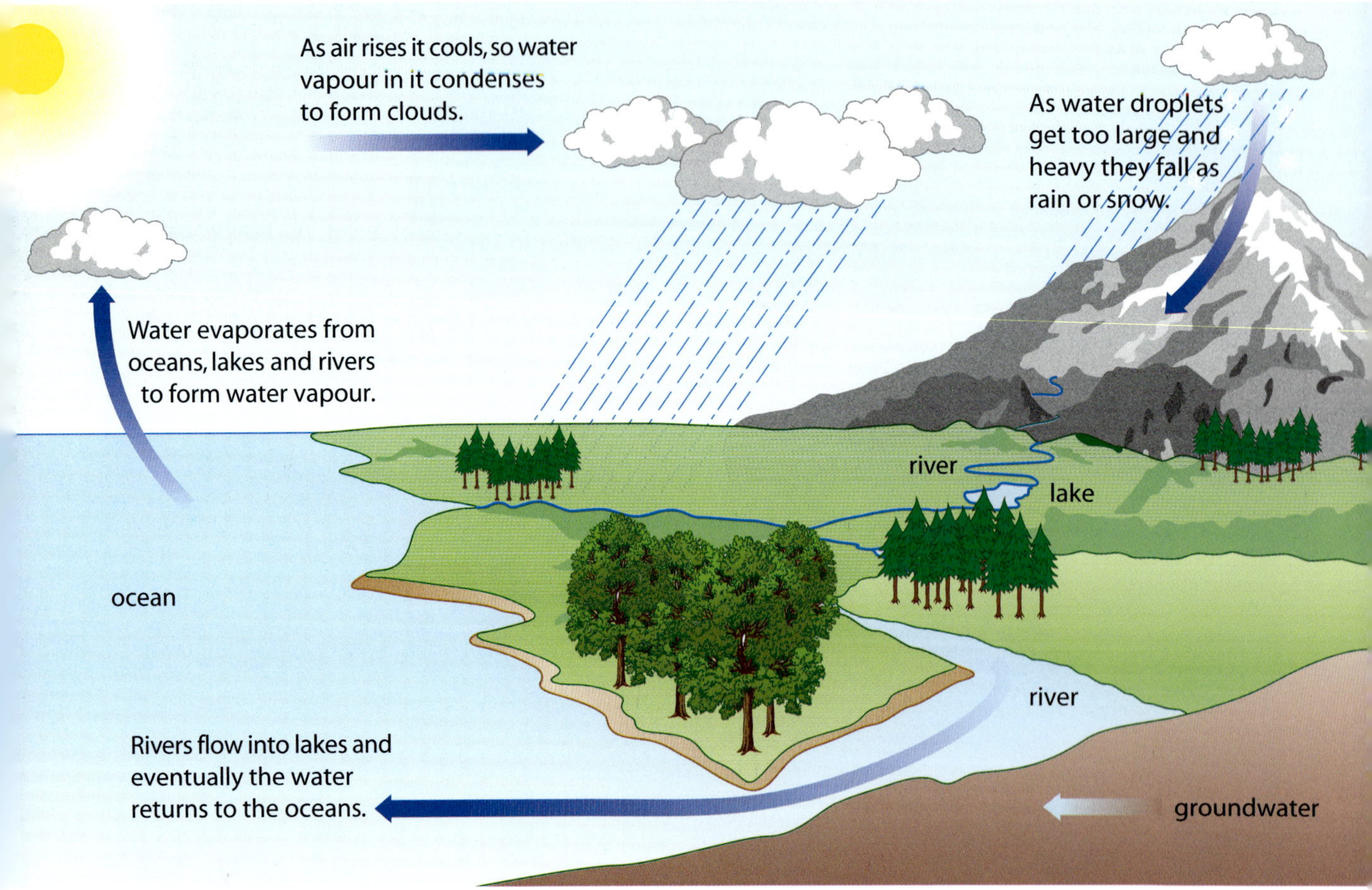

The water cycle

The children were drinking from cans. The cans were straight from the fridge. The children noticed liquid collecting on the cold cans. The liquid was running down the cans. Some of the children thought the cans were leaking. Were they right? What was happening?

Temperature is a **measure** of how hot or cold things are. Thermometers measure temperature. A hot shower has more heat in it than a candle flame. But the candle flame is hotter. It is at a higher temperature.

A **thermometer** measures temperatures in degrees. There are many different temperature scales. The most important scale was devised by Anders Celsius. We call it the Celsius scale. Temperatures are measured in degrees Celsius, or °C.

On the Celsius scale, a hot shower might be 40 degrees Celsius (40°C). A candle flame is 800 degrees Celsius (800°C). Although there is more heat in the shower, the candle is at a much higher temperature.

Which is at a higher temperature, a bowl of hot soup or a **firework**?

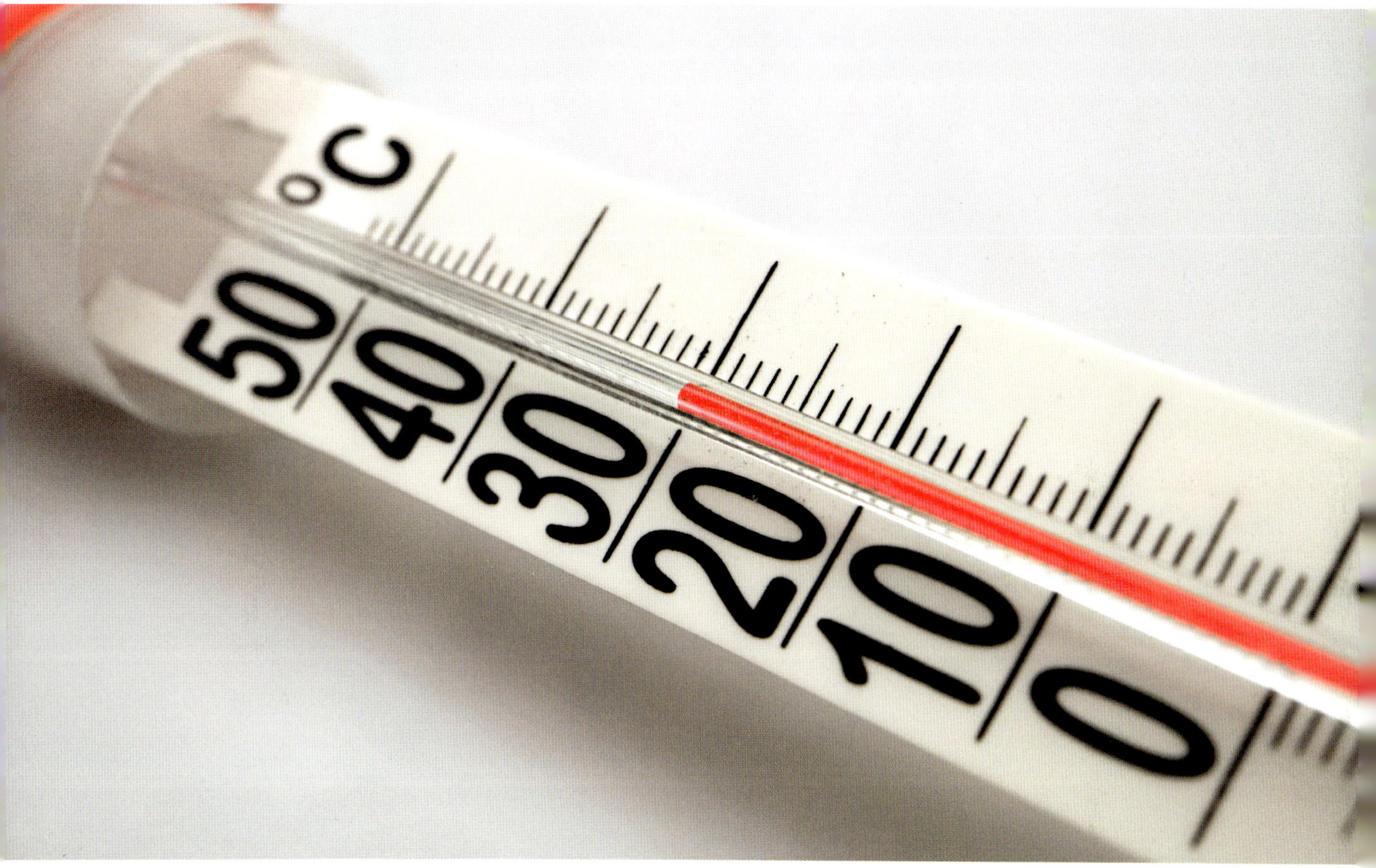

There are different types of thermometer. A glass thermometer is a **tube** containing a liquid. Liquids expand when they are warmed. The warmer the liquid in the tube, the more space the liquid takes up. The expanding liquid pushes up the narrow tube.

You can read the temperature of the liquid on a scale on the side of the thermometer. Can you read the temperature on this scale?

Some thermometers work because metals **expand** when they are heated. Different metals expand at different **rates**. A **strip** made from two pieces of different metals bends as it gets hotter. The hotter it is, the more it bends. The bending metal can move a **needle**.

Fever strips work because **crystals** in them change with the temperature.

Anders Celsius was from Sweden. He lived 300 years ago. He made a temperature scale based on the freezing and boiling of water. The **boiling point** of water was set at 100°C. The **freezing point** was set at 0°C. The C is for Celsius.

The boiling point of pure water is 100 degrees Celsius (100°C). At boiling point, the bubbling water is losing water vapour.

If you go on boiling the water, it will all become vapour. No water will be left.

What happens if you go on heating water at its boiling point? It will not get any hotter. Once it has reached 100°C, the water stays at that temperature. As it boils, more water vapour is lost. No matter how hard you heat it, the water will not get any hotter.

The freezing point of pure water is zero degrees Celsius. (0°C). At freezing point, the water becomes ice. If you go on freezing the water, it will not get any colder until it is all ice. Anders Celsius divided the scale between the freezing and boiling points of water into degrees. We use these degrees to measure temperature.

A temperature of 40°C is hotter than a temperature of 20°C.

In some countries, it rains and snows in the winter. Water freezes in the cold weather. The roads become icy and **slippery**. People put salt on the road to melt the ice. The freezing point of salt water is lower than the freezing point of pure water. Unless it gets very cold, the salt water on the road will not freeze.

Some solids **dissolve** when they are added to water. The solid and the water become one material. The solid is in every part of the water. Stirring speeds up dissolving. Heating speeds up dissolving. The solid and liquid become a **solution**.

Adding instant coffee to water makes a solution. You can see the brown coffee mixed with the water. Adding sugar or salt to water makes a solution. The solution is **transparent**. You cannot see the sugar or salt, but you can taste it.

It is not possible to **sieve** a solid out of a solution. Even a **filter** will not separate the solid from the liquid.

Evaporation is when water droplets leave the surface of water. Evaporation can be speeded up. Evaporation is faster when the water is heated. The water droplets move more, and leave easily. Evaporation is faster when a wind blows across water. Droplets are carried away quickly.

Evaporation separates solids from water. Droplets of water leave the surface when water evaporates. But the solids do not leave the solution. When all the water has gone, the solid is left behind. Salt, sugar or instant coffee can be recovered from the solution. This picture shows the bottom of a lake after the water has evaporated.

The children put water in three different containers. One container was tall and thin. Another was wide and flat. The third container was between these two in shape. They put the same amount of water in each container. They put the containers in a warm place.

The children checked the containers each day. They found that the water evaporated from each container. One by one, the containers became empty. All the water had evaporated. The water evaporated fastest from the wide, flat container.

Why do you think the water evaporated fastest from this container?

Activity

Spelling test

This can be done in pairs or small teams.

Preparation: Choose 15 new and/or difficult words from this book. One person/team then reads out the word and asks another person/team to spell it. This can be done as a speaking test or writing test.

Scoring: The person/team that reads out the words gets one point for each word correctly pronounced. They also get a point if the other person/team gets the spelling incorrect. The person/team doing the spelling gets one point for each correct spelling.

Glossary

boiling point: the temperature when a liquid becomes a gas

condensation: gas becoming liquid

crystals: small regular-shaped pieces of a substance, formed naturally when this substance becomes solid

dissolve: if something solid dissolves, it becomes part of a liquid when you mix it with the liquid

evaporation: a liquid changing to a gas

expand: to become larger in size, number or amount

filter: to separate a solid from a liquid using a fine sieve

firework: an object that you light so that it explodes and produces bright lights in the sky

freezing point: the temperature at which a liquid becomes a solid

measure: a way of testing or judging something

needle: a small thin piece of metal on a scientific instrument that moves backwards and forwards and points to numbers or directions

rates: the speed at which something happens

sieve: a round wire tool for separating small objects from large objects

slippery: something that is slippery is difficult to walk on or hold because it is wet, oily or covered in ice

solution: when a solid has spread through a liquid

strip: long narrow piece of something

thermometer: a piece of equipment that measures the temperature of the air, of your body and so on

tube: round pipe made of metal, glass and so on, especially for liquids or gases to go through

water vapour: drops of water in the air

transparent: if something is transparent, you can see through it